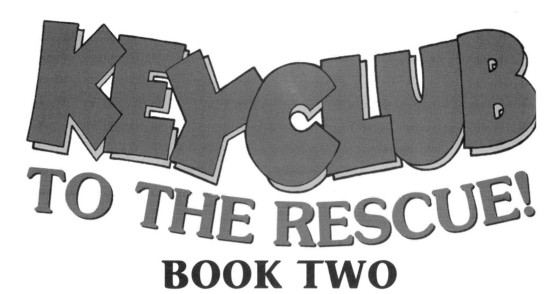

CW00421849

TO THE RESCUE!
BOOK TWO

by Ann Bryant

for Sue Mahon, sight-reader par excellence

Editor
Louisa Wallace

Cover design by
John Good Holbrook Ltd.

Illustrations by
Paul Selvey, John Good Holbrook Ltd.

Music Setting by
Barnes Music Engraving Ltd.

Published 2001

International MUSIC Publications

© **International Music Publications Ltd.**
Griffin House, 161 Hammersmith Road
London W6 8BS
England

Caring for the Environment
This book has been produced with special regard to the environment. We have insisted on the use of acid-free, neutral-sized paper made from pulps which have not been elemental bleached and have sought assurance that the pulp is farmed from sustainable forests.

About this book...

The pieces in **KEYCLUB TO THE RESCUE BOOK TWO** are designed as reinforcement for **KEYCLUB BOOK TWO,** helping your pupils overcome troublesome patches whilst developing and maintaining sight-reading skills.

As in Book One, all the pieces are short, repetitive and almost entirely free of fingerings, which helps train the pupil to look ahead. There are no dynamics, tempo indications or expression marks, making it easier to concentrate on the notes. Each new note appears in the same Keyland area as it does in the tutor book. Words are introduced during the first part of the book to help the pupil identify and grasp the rhythms, and to highlight the importance of keeping the music flowing along.

All the common chord shapes and hand positions for this level are used so the pieces can be mastered easily and the book revisited time and time again as a sight-reading aid. But there is none of the dryness of typical sight-reading guides here, just all the fun of the Keyclub series with a whole wealth of Keyland characters, familiar and new!

CONTENTS

Rocket

Paddy the Pancake Man

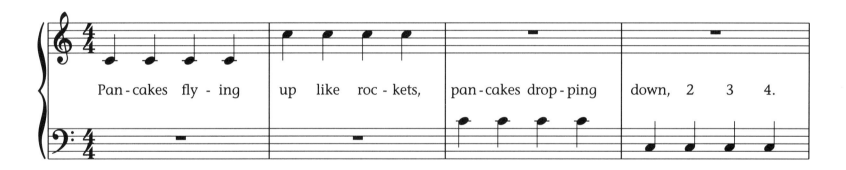

Pan-cakes fly - ing | up like roc - kets, | pan-cakes drop-ping | down, 2 3 4.

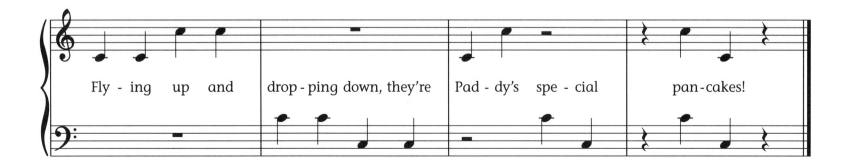

Fly - ing up and | drop-ping down, they're | Pad - dy's spe - cial | pan-cakes!

Wanda Wings the Waitress

Wan-da Wings the wait-ress, Wan-da Wings the wait-ress flies a-round the ca-fé. Here! There! Here! There!

Wan-da Wings the wait-ress, Wan-da Wings the wait-ress flies a-round the ca - fé. Eve-ry-where!

Bessy the Bossy Chef

Slosher the Washer Upper

Bonzo the Lobster

Bon - zo the Lob - ster, Bon - zo the Lob - ster,

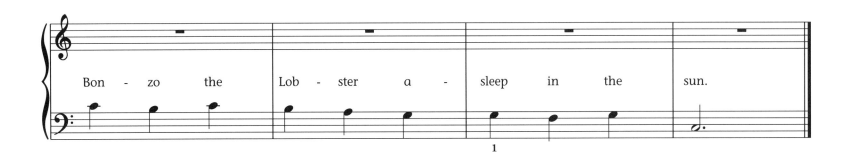

Bon - zo the Lob - ster a - sleep in the sun.

1

Fergus Flat Fish (trying to wake Bonzo up)

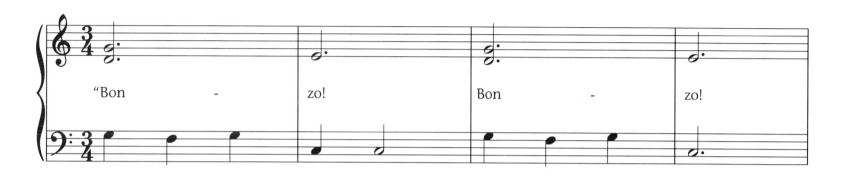

"Bon - zo! Bon - zo!

Bon - zo! Bon - zo!"

Patti the Octopus

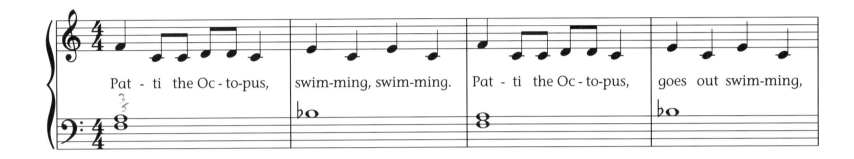

Pat - ti the Oc - to-pus, | swim-ming, swim-ming. | Pat - ti the Oc - to-pus, | goes out swim-ming,

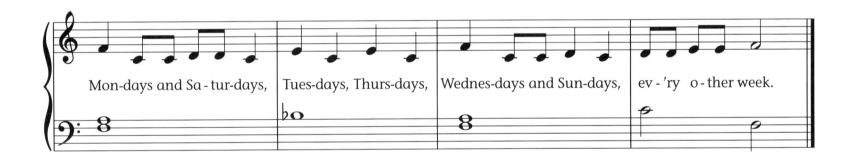

Mon-days and Sa - tur-days, | Tues-days, Thurs-days, | Wednes-days and Sun-days, | ev - 'ry o - ther week.

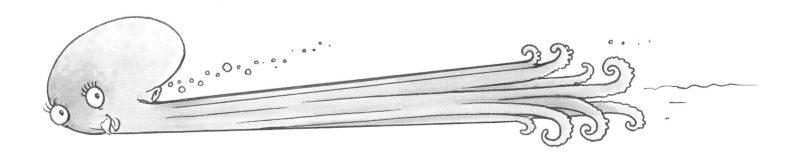

Whoosh-along-Walt

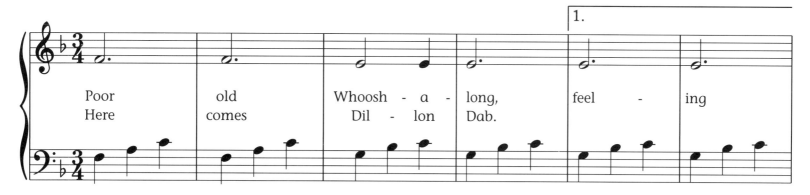

Poor old Whoosh - a - long, feel - ing
Here comes Dil - lon Dab.

sick!

"Stop pre-tend-ing, Whoosh, be quick!"

⑪

Kangaroo Jump

Kevin Kangaroo
(loses his way and shows up in the Wild Woods)

"This place looks nice!" Ke - vin Kan - ga - roo jumped for joy!

"That's a high jump, Ke - vin," said a rab - bit called Roy.

Wilbur Wolf (worn out)

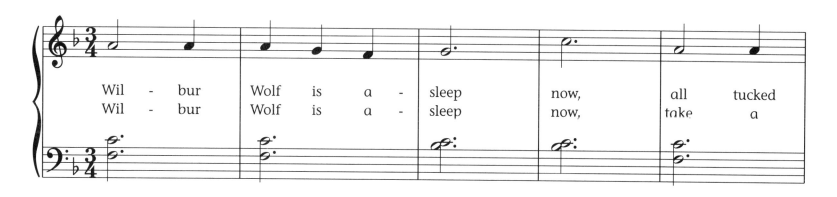

Wil - bur Wolf is a - sleep now, all tucked
Wil - bur Wolf is a - sleep now, take a

1. up in his lair.

2. peep if you dare!

Sergeant Stoat

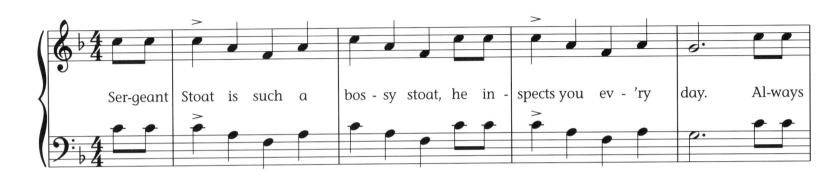

Ser-geant Stoat is such a bos-sy stoat, he in - spects you ev - 'ry day. Al-ways

smart and clean for the Wild Wood scene, he in - sists you must o - bey!

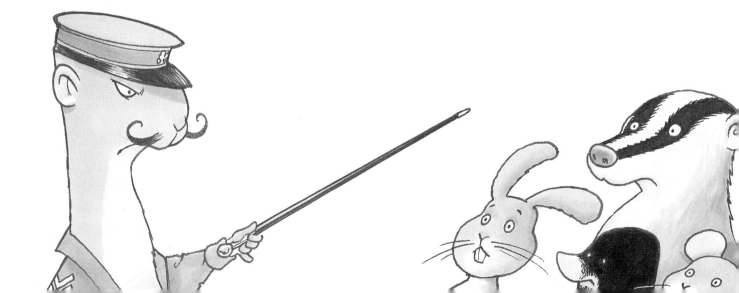

Mrs Bear

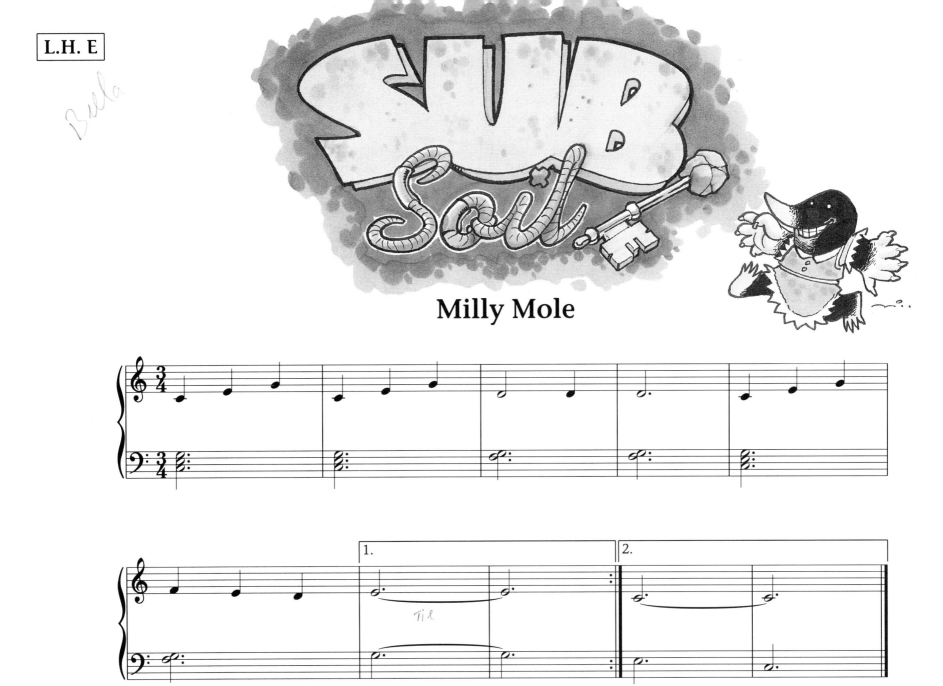

Milly Mole

Martin Mole

Rocky Mole

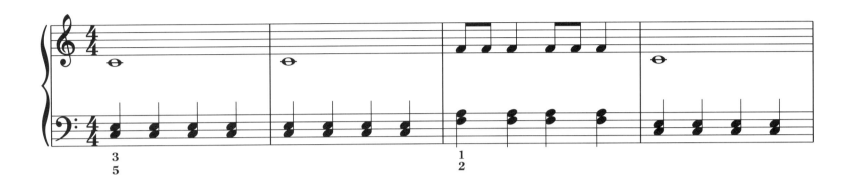

Use given L.H. fingerings or simply use $\frac{3}{5}$ for L.H. chords throughout.

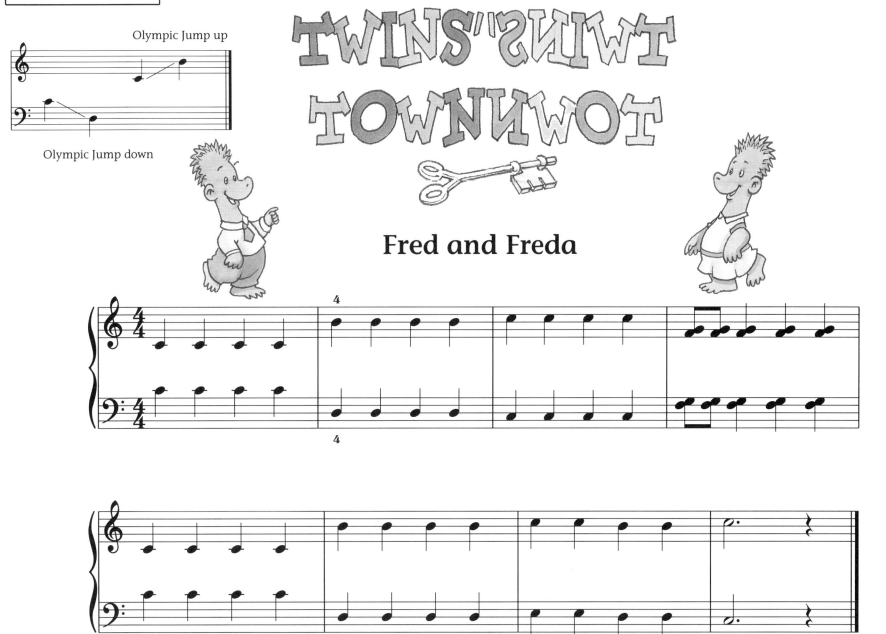

L.H. D & R.H. B

Olympic Jump up

Olympic Jump down

Fred and Freda

Sonja and Serena Step

Horace and Hatty Harmony

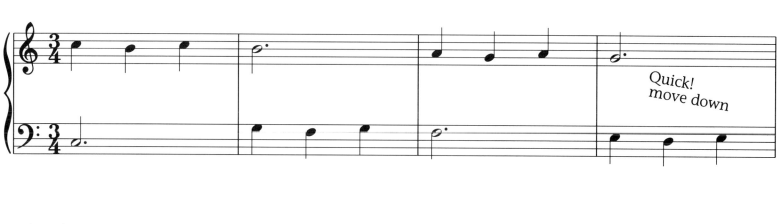

Quick!
move down

21

Carly Chord and Miranda Melody

Kelly Ann and Emma Jane

Danny and Delilah D

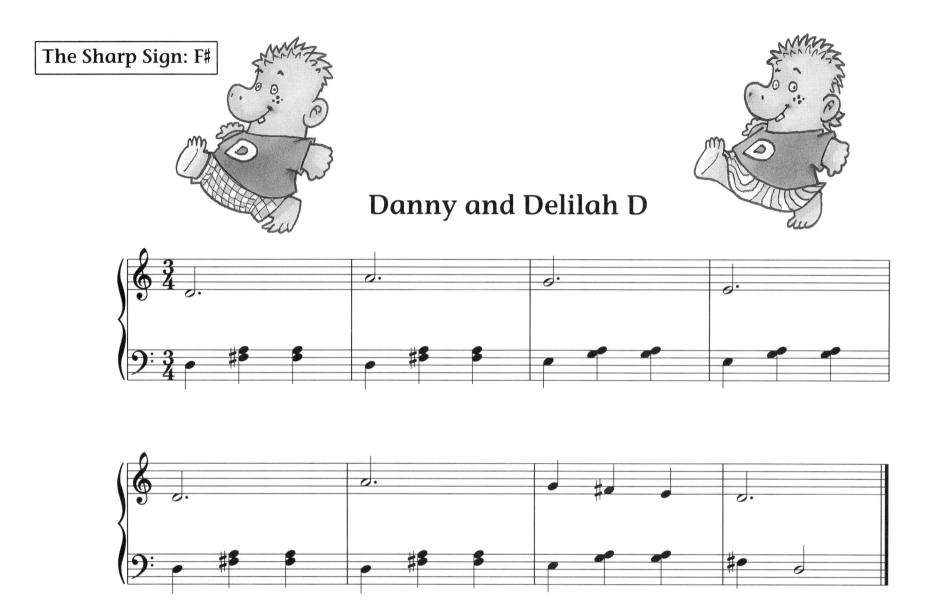

Learn this piece by heart. You'll see why when you do the next piece!

Transposition

Now try playing the previous piece in C position and F position.
We've given you the first four bars of each!

Invent names for the C twins and the F twins!

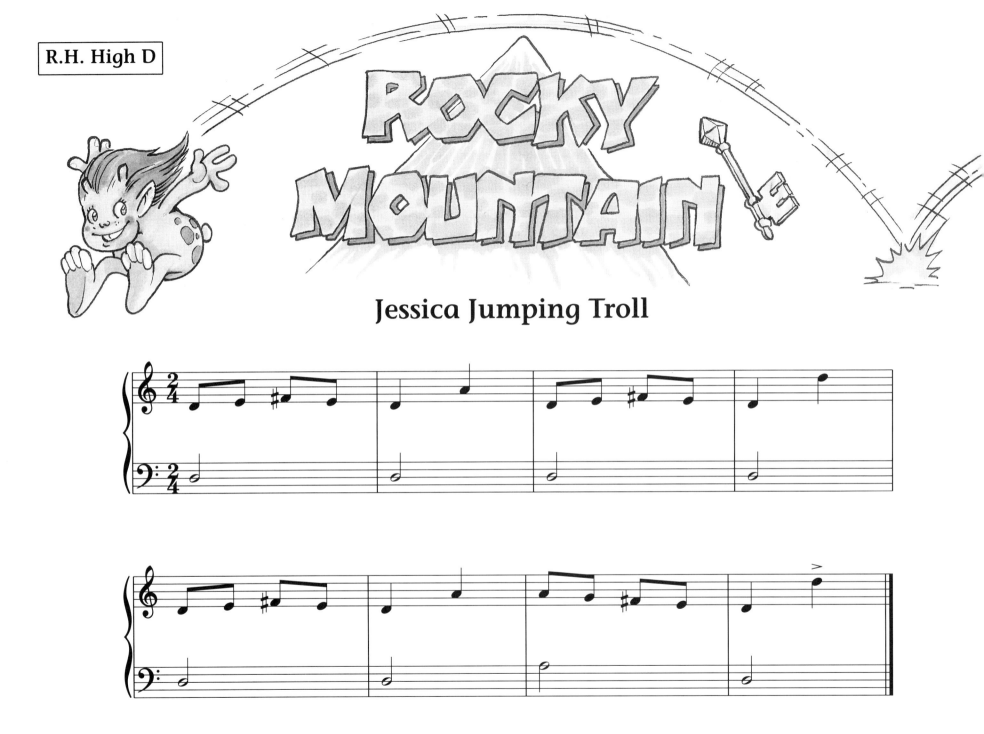

Jessica Jumping Troll

Tilly Troll

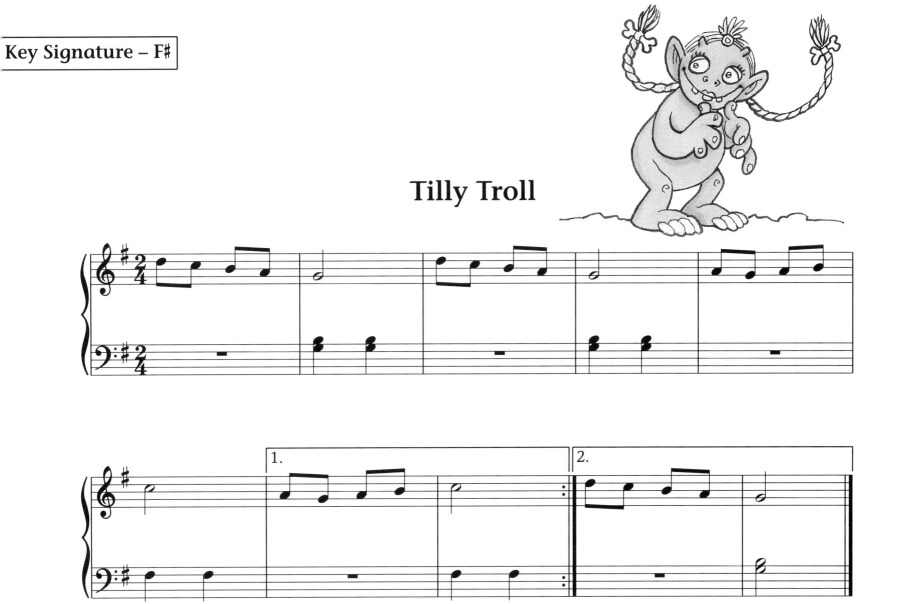

Major the Marching Troll

Tobias Top Troll

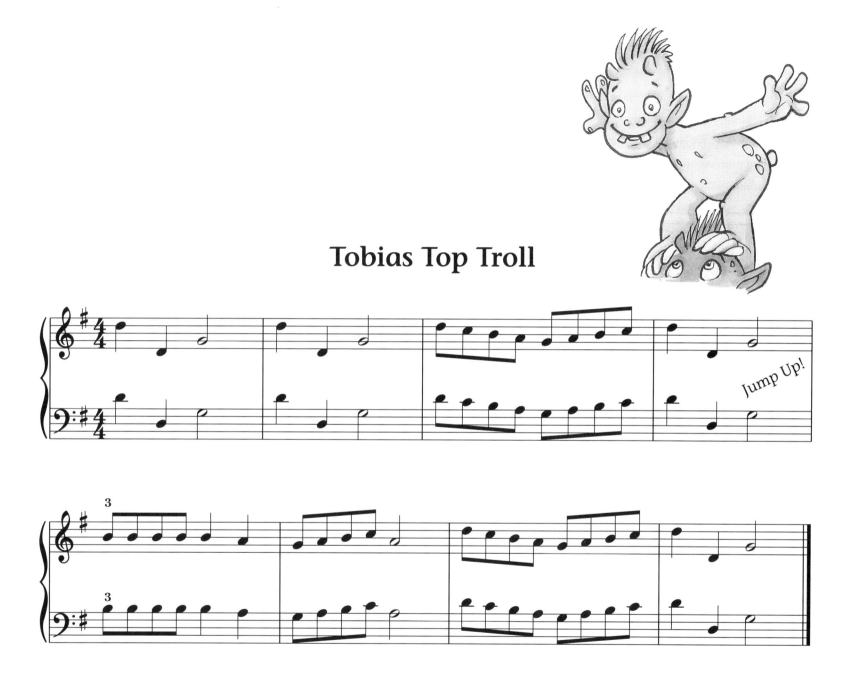

Jump Up!

Learn this piece by heart so you can look at your hands!

Scat the Skating Troll

Ferogo the Frog Troll
(Work out why he's the **frog** troll)

Princess Poppy (Pete's bride)

King Pete the Cheat!

Baby Billy (keeps running away!)

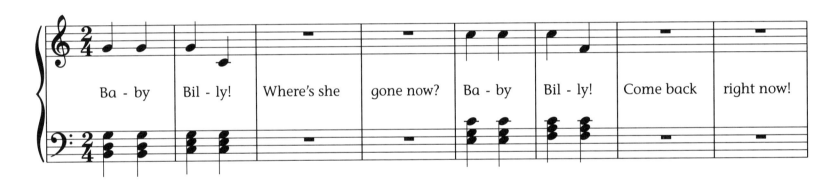

Ba - by Bil - ly! Where's she gone now? Ba - by Bil - ly! Come back right now!

Ba - by Bil - ly! This is se - ri - ous! There you are, you naugh - ty girl!

The Keyclub Rap

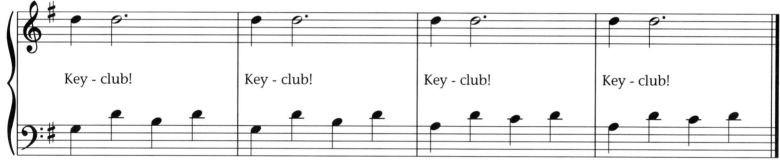

D.C. al Fine

Printed and bound in Great Britain 4/01

by Ann Bryant

Ref: 3582A

Ref: 3583A

Ref: 3584A

Ref: 5469A

Ref: 5470A

Ref: 5471A

Ref: 5847A

EVERY YOUNG PERSON'S FIRST PIANO COURSE

At last a piano course that's up to date, fun to use and packed with pieces to play, things to do and stickers to stick! The KEYCLUB Course takes place in Keyland – a magical fantasy world of characters and places. KEYCLUB however, is more than just a piano course.
It's a real kids' club that every young person can join!

KEYCLUB More Than Just a Piano Course